New
ADVENTURES
IN MANDARIN CHINESE
Volume 1
FIRST REVISION

The Fox and The Goat
Sam SONG

Publicity

To request the author for an interview or for
an appearance at an event (conference,
speaking engagement, etc.), please email
samsong.author@gmail.com
or telephone +886-927-838562

Acknowledgements

Special thanks and love to John Paul, Carol Creed, Frederick Reeves, Jordan Smith, Matt Flint, Kathy Christensen, George FERRANTE, Anthony BIANCARDI, Craig Zaidel, Christian BOGUE, Melissa KAWA, DeAnna Walton, Mrs. Lockett, Soniz RUIZ, Juanita Moreland, Shane and Tammy Carpenter, Jean Strauss, S. W. SONG, Lindsey Lou Lichfield, J. SONG, J. Chen

SS

~ **Contents** ~

Introduction

~ **Contents** ~

~ **Contents** ~

*After studying through this book,
you will be able to read
the famous fable
"The Fox 🦊 and The Goat 🐐"
in Chinese to your children,
students, friends, and colleagues!
They will be amazed!*

Chinese Character Practice Sheet (Example)

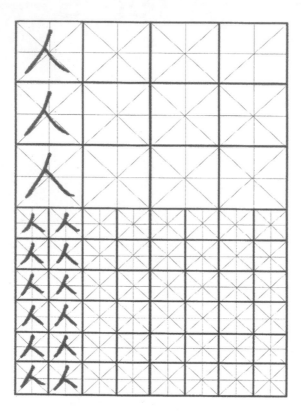

This is a handwritten representation of the Chinese character that means "person". Please use the boxes to write this character the best you can. You will find it helpful to continue writing out new characters at least three times when you come across them in this book.

Introduction

Chinese character

Chinese speakers consider a "Chinese character" to be a word since it represents a complete concept just like English words do, while most English speakers refer to it as a "Chinese Character". So for the purposes of keeping things simple and avoiding any confusion, this book will use the term "Chinese character" throughout.

Memorizing Chinese characters

It's better for readers to draw, or write, each new character at least 3 times in order to memorize it while reading the book. Chinese primary school students do this all the time, and hundreds of millions of Chinese learn Chinese characters successfully. Surely you will be successful too.

Writing Chinese characters

Learning to write Chinese characters by hand is one of the best ways to gain a thorough understanding of each character. Chinese characters consist of strokes that are usually written in a specific order.

The most important rule to follow when writing strokes is: Horizontal strokes are written from left to right and vertical strokes are written from top to bottom.

 This shows an outline character, 走, shown in the book. The numbers illustrate the sequence of the strokes.

Every stroke has two ends and as a general rule the location of the number on or around the stroke shows which end the stroke starts. For example, ⌐, 5 is on the left side of the stroke, and ⌐ shows the stroke is written from left to right.

The following diagram shows how to write the character stroke by stroke.

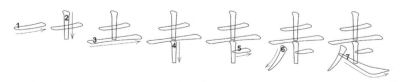

Traditional and simplified characters

The Chinese traditional written characters have existed for over 5,000 years, and some Chinese characters have been simplified by common usage.

In an attempt to increase literacy, starting in the 1950s, the government of China decided to include some simplified characters in the official written language, and it has even made a few new simplified characters available, although many traditional characters were left untouched in that process. (**Also it's essential to point out that the spoken language, Mandarin, remains the same.**) As a result, **<u>the written Chinese characters used in China are called "simplified Chinese characters" or "simplified Chinese.</u>**" Generally speaking, simplified characters are currently used worldwide, though many people outside of China still use what is called "traditional Chinese characters," or "traditional Chinese."

Please note, for the most commonly used Chinese characters, simplified Chinese characters keep more than 70% of the traditional Chinese characters.

Pinyin – Chinese pronunciation

Pinyin is the Romanized system used to represent the pronunciation of Chinese characters. Pinyin uses the same alphabets as English, though Pinyin also uses the extra letter 'ü' and four tone marks. Pinyin is very useful for those who are learning Chinese and is used in China and throughout the world.

In this book, next to new Chinese characters, you may notice Roman characters. Below is an example:

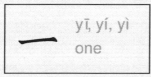

"yī, yí, yì" is the Pinyin, or pronunciation, of the Chinese character "一," which means "one" in Chinese.

At the end of the book, there is a Pronunciation Reference, with Mandarin phonetic symbols, for all Chinese characters from the book.

Download audio files

www.discoverChinese.cn
Author email samsong.author@gmail.com

Please download audio files at the author site above. So, while reading the book, you can listen to the pronunciation of Chinese, character by character, phrase by phrase, sentence by sentence, and finally the complete story of The Fox and The Goat.

(As a new learner of Chinese, you may want to concentrate your attention on recognizing Chinese characters.)

Story approach to learn Chinese

Contextual learning is very important and one of the best ways to learn Chinese. That's one of the reasons why this book takes a story approach to introduce Chinese characters.

Conventions used in this book

In this book, "traditional Chinese" means, "traditional Chinese characters," while "simplified Chinese" means "simplified Chinese characters."

"Chinese" refers to both "traditional Chinese characters" and "simplified Chinese characters."

Chinese characters often have several different meanings, usages, or even pronunciations depending on the context or the combination with other characters. In this book, generally, only relevant meanings, usages, or even pronunciations are presented. To learn more meanings, usages, or pronunciations for a specific Chinese character, please consult a proper Chinese dictionary.

The Fox and The Goat

狐狸 与 山羊

狐狸 與 山羊

Unveil
the foundation of
Chinese characters!

Chinese Character Practice Sheet (Sample)

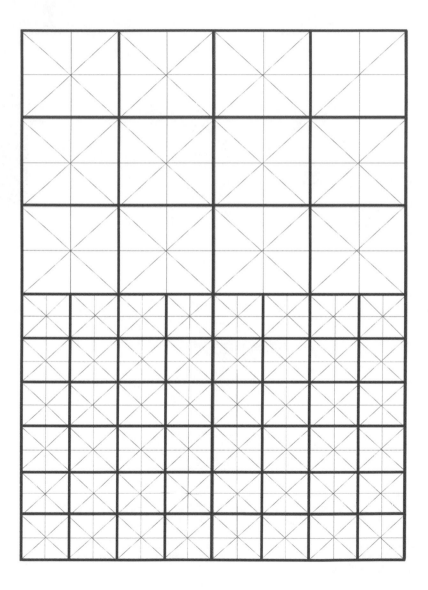

一 yī, yí, yì
one

Have you ever thought about how easy some Chinese characters could be? Here are three examples.

It is easy to learn that **one** is 一, **two** is 二, and **three** is 三 in Chinese.

For a long time, the Chinese have adopted and used the Arabic numbers, such as 1, 2, and 3 as Chinese numbers. Also, when used as a number, 一 and 1, 二 and 2, 三 and 3 are often used interchangeably in Chinese by the general public.

English	one	two	three
Chinese	一	二	三
	1	2	3

There is no difference in 一, 二, and 三 between traditional Chinese and simplified Chinese.

From this point on in this book, I will mention the simplified Chinese character only if it is different from the traditional Chinese character. In most cases, they are identical.

4   The Fox 🦊 and The Goat 🐐

TC: Traditional Chinese   SC: Simplified Chinese

TC	SC	Pinyin	TC	SC	Pinyin
一		yī, yí, yì	二		èr, liǎng
三		sān			

As a general rule, 一 is pronounced yī as an ordinary number, but when 一 precedes a fourth tone Chinese character, 一 is pronounced yí, otherwise, 一 is pronounced yì.
(Beginners sometimes speak Mandarin using the wrong tones. Even so, they usually still can be understood by most Chinese as long as they speak Mandarin at a slower speed.)

** *Generally, "2" is pronounced èr, though "2" also can be pronounced liǎng orally when "2" is followed by a classifier.* A classifier is a word, such as 隻 or 只 on the next page, that denotes the form or shape of an item.

You have learned (Simplified Chinese):

一 二 三

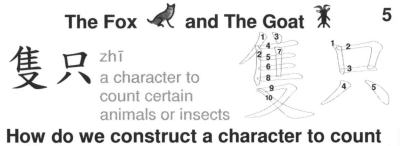

隻只　zhī
a character to
count certain
animals or insects

**How do we construct a character to count
animals in Chinese? Let's look at a bird
sketch first!**

🐦 shows a sketch of a bird, and 隹 shows a
sketch of a bird with a short tail, according to
ancient Chinese literature.

屮, 乂, or 乄 shows a sketch of a hand.
Let's use the progression
乂 ➡ 乂 ➡ 又 or 又

to reach the symbol, 又, that symbolizes a
hand here.

隻 shows a bird captured by a hand.
Let's use the progression
隻 ➡ 隻 ➡ 隻 ➡ 隻

to reach the character, 隻 zhī, that is used as a
character to count animals or insects, such as,
a dog, a cat, a bear, a bird, a duck, etc.
隻 is a traditional Chinese character.

To make the simplified Chinese for this character 隻, we simply take the "又" part of it, and find the similar shape 只 to represent it. Therefore, 隻 is 只 in simplified Chinese.

Please note as a general rule the pronunciation of the traditional Chinese and the simplified Chinese for the same character is the same.

Therefore, 隻 and 只 have the same pronunciation, zhī, and the same meaning.

一隻 is 一只 in simplified Chinese.

一隻 or 一只 is pronounced yì zhī, because 一 precedes a first tone Chinese character 隻 or 只.

You have learned (Simplified Chinese):
一只

狐狸 hú lí
fox

How do we construct Chinese characters that mean "fox" in Chinese? Let's observe "a sitting fox" first!

shows a brief sketch of a sitting fox. Let's use the progression

瓜 → 瓜 → 瓜 → 瓜

to reach the symbol, 瓜*, that symbolizes a "fox" here.

shows a sketch of a sitting animal. Let's use the progression

→ → 犭

to reach the symbol, 犭, that symbolizes "some kinds of animals that look like 🐾 while sitting." When 犭 is used as a component of a Chinese character, it symbolizes this character is related to "some kinds of animals that look like 🐾 while sitting," such as the following 狐.

The Fox 🦊 **and The Goat** 🐐

By putting 犭 and 瓜 together, 狐 hú means "fox" in Chinese.

However, to avoid employing a one-syllable character in speech, there is a need to construct another character to go with 狐 to mean "fox."

Here, 🐾 depicts an animal from a distance. Let's use the progression

畟 ➔ 畢 ➔ 里 ➔ 里

to reach the symbol, 里 lǐ, that symbolizes an animal which looks like a fox.

Now, by putting 犭 and 里 together, 狸 lí means an animal, that looks like a fox, but with a smaller body and long, thick tail.

By putting 狐 and 狸 together, 狐狸 hú lí is selected to mean "fox" in modern oral and written Chinese.

狐 also means "fox" in written Chinese, though 狐 is also used with other character(s) to form a phrase or term in Chinese.

As a general rule, Chinese nouns, such as 狐狸, do not change at all between their singular and plural forms.

Below are the correct forms:

English	one fox	two foxes	three foxes
Traditional Chinese	一隻狐狸	二隻狐狸	三隻狐狸
	1 隻狐狸	2 隻狐狸	3 隻狐狸
Simplified Chinese	一只狐狸	二只狐狸	三只狐狸
	1 只狐狸	2 只狐狸	3 只狐狸

*Also, ⚫ shows a sketch of a creeping plant bearing an edible fruit.
Let's use the progression

🍈 ➜ 🍈 ➜ 瓜 ➜ 瓜

to reach the symbol, 瓜 guā, that means a large edible fruit (some of which are considered vegetables), including melons, squash, cucumbers, etc. In other words, melon, squash, or cucumber is one kind of 瓜 in Chinese.

* guā *is onomatopoeia, originating from the sound of a* 瓜 *hitting the ground and breaking.*

You have learned (Simplified Chinese):
一只狐狸 A Fox

不   bù, bú
       no; not

How do we construct a character that means "no" in Chinese? Let's first look at how ancient Chinese told the future!

In ancient China, to make decisions fortunetellers could apply an external heat source to a turtle shell and the shell may crack. Fortunetellers would then observe the appearance of the cracks to tell the future.

Some cracks looked like ├ bǔ , that means "to divine" in Chinese. If two consecutive ├ failed to get a positive answer from the gods, it symbolized "no."

Let's use the progression

├├ ➜ ⊤├ ➜ ⊤├ ➜ 不 ➜ 不

to reach the character, 不 bù or bú, that means "no" or "not" in Chinese.

When 不 goes before a fourth-toned Chinese character in a phrase, 不 is pronounced bú.

Otherwise, 不 is pronounced bù.

You have learned:

一只狐狸 A Fox   不

走 zǒu
to walk

How do we construct a character to express "to walk" in Chinese? Let's look at a foot first!

 shows a sketch of a foot. Let's use the progression

🦶 ➜ 止 ➜ 止

to reach the symbol, **止**, that symbolizes "to walk" here.

大 can be used to symbolize the long stride of a person walking. Also, 大 can be presented as 土. So, by putting 大 on top of 止, we get 走 or 走, that symbolizes "a person stretching out two legs to walk." Therefore, 走 zǒu means "to walk" in Chinese.

You have learned:
一只狐狸 A Fox   不走

The Fox  and The Goat

運运 yùn
luck; fate

How do we construct a character that means "luck" in Chinese? Let's construct a character to mean "vehicle" first!

or shows the tire and axle, two key components of a vehicle.
Let's use the progression

to reach the character, 車 chē, that means

"vehicle." 車 is a traditional Chinese character.

車 is 车 in simplified Chinese.

Army vehicles in a surrounding military

maneuver, , were often seen on the ancient battlefield.
Let's use the progression

to reach the character, 軍 jūn, that means

"army." 軍 is a traditional Chinese character.

軍 is 军 in simplified Chinese.

辶 or 辶 shows a person or a subject moving so fast that it leaves a dust trail behind him or it.

By putting 辶 and 軍 together, 運 yùn shows "an army moving very fast", so, 運 means "to transport" or "transportation." Also, while sitting in a vehicle moving very fast, we may pray for "good **luck**", so 運 is also used to mean "luck" or "fate." 運 is a traditional Chinese character. 運 is 运 in simplified Chinese.

Chinese characters often go together (or in pairs) to form a meaning. Here, 走運 is a good example and "walk or transportation in ancient times" is very much related to "*luck*", so, 走運 zǒu yùn means "to have good luck" or "to be very fortunate."

English	not	lucky	unlucky
Traditional Chinese	不	走運	不走運
Simplified Chinese		走运	不走运

You have learned:
一只狐狸 A Fox   不走运 unlucky

的 de
    possessive symbol;
    adjective symbol

How do we construct a Chinese character to express "possession?" Let's look at English grammar first!

In English, one way to form a possessive meaning is to add an apostrophe and an s at the end of a noun.

In Chinese, **the character 的 is simply added** to a noun, a phrase, or a pronoun to form a possessive meaning. How?

Let me share a story with you first:

Bill needed some food so he asked his friend **John** for help. Later that night, John arrived carrying a light in his right hand and some food in his left hand. Let's see how this applies:

◐ shows a sketch of a light.

Let's use the progression ◐ ➜ 白 ➜ 白

to reach the character, 白 bái, which

symbolizes "light" initially, and 白 means "white" in Chinese.

勺 or 勹 shows a sketch of a scoop and 勺 is the modification of a scoop with a dot which symbolizes food or something inside the scoop. So, 勺 sháo, means "scoop" in Chinese. 勺 symbolizes "food" here.

Now, by putting 白 and 勺 together, 的 de is an illustration to describe the scene in the above story.

Perhaps the ending scene of the story would be John giving Bill the food and saying, "It's **yours**."

The story helps us understand the character 的 expresses "possession" in Chinese.

Therefore, we add the character 的 to a pronoun or noun to indicate possession.

The Fox 🦊 **and The Goat** 🐐

English	a lucky fox	two lucky foxes
Traditional Chinese	一隻走運的狐狸	二隻走運的狐狸
Simplified Chinese	一只走运的狐狸	二只走运的狐狸

As we mentioned earlier: *"When* 不 *goes before a fourth-toned Chinese character as a phrase,* 不 *is pronounced as* bú. *Otherwise,* 不 *is pronounced as* bù.*"*

Here, 走 zǒu *is a third-toned character, therefore,* in the following phrases, 不走運 or 不走运 is pronounced bù zǒu yùn.

English	an unlucky fox	two unlucky foxes
Traditional Chinese	一隻不走運的狐狸	二隻不走運的狐狸
Simplified Chinese	一只不走运的狐狸	二只不走运的狐狸

You have learned:
一只不走运的狐狸，
An unlucky Fox

小 xiǎo
small

How do we construct a character that means "small" in Chinese? Let's observe the "falling rain" first!

/// shows a sketch of rain falling.

/√/ shows a sketch of rain falling with a bouncing raindrop.

Let's use the progression

/√/ ➔ 小

to reach the character, 小 xiǎo.
We all know that rain is very small droplets of water, so, 小 has been selected to mean "small" in Chinese.

You have learned:
一只不走运的狐狸，不小

心 xīn
heart; mind

How do we construct a character that means "heart" or "mind" in Chinese? Let's observe a heart first!

shows a sketch of a heart.
Let's use the progression

to reach the symbol, 心 or 忄.

心 xīn means "heart" in Chinese.

忄 symbolizes "mind" in Chinese, because culturally Chinese people associate the heart with "the source of thinking" or "mind." 忄 is usually used as a component of a Chinese character. An example will be displayed later in the book.

The ancient Chinese people imagined that their hearts might become smaller when suddenly facing danger. Accordingly, 小心 xiǎo xīn has been selected to mean "cautious" in Chinese. 不小心 bù xiǎo xīn means "incautious" in Chinese.

失 shī
to lose

How do we construct a character that means "to lose" in Chinese? Let's look at a hand first!

业 shows a sketch of a hand.
Let's use the progression

业 → 屮 → 屮 → 屮

to reach the symbol, 屮, that symbolizes a hand here.

失 symbolizes that a hand held something then lost it.   Let's use the progression

失 → 失

to reach the character, 失 shī, means "to lose" in Chinese.

You have learned:
一只不走运的狐狸，不小心失
An unlucky Fox, incautiously lost

The Fox 🦊 and The Goat 🐐

足 zú
foot

How do we construct a character that means "foot" in Chinese? Let's observe a foot!

shows a sketch of a foot.
Let's use the progression

👣 → 𧿹 → 足 → 足 → 疋

to reach the character, 足 zú that means "foot"

in Chinese. 疋 symbolizes a foot, and 疋 is often used as a component of a character.

English	lose	foot	to lose one's footing
Traditional Chinese	失	足	失足
Simplified Chinese			

You have learned:
一只不走运的狐狸，不小心失足
An unlucky Fox, incautiously lost its footing

掉 diào
to fall; to drop

How do we construct a character that means "to fall" in Chinese? Let's look at a scene first!

an arm and hand ——
—— a person
—— a ball
—— a desk

The above scene shows a person standing on a ball. The ball is on a desk, and a hand is pushing the ball. Therefore, this person may fall or drop at any moment.

凵 shows a sketch of an arm and hand.
Let's use the progression

凵 ➜ 丁 ➜ 扌 ➜ 扌

to reach the symbol, 扌, which symbolizes a "hand" when used as a component of a character.
Let's use the progression

➜ 掉 ➜ 掉 ➜ 掉

to reach the character, 掉 diào, which means "to fall" or "to drop" in Chinese.

You have learned:

一只不走运的狐狸，不小心失足掉

An unlucky Fox incautiously lost its footing and fell

The Fox 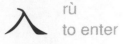 **and The Goat**

入 rù
to enter

How do we construct a character that means "to enter" in Chinese? Let's look at a plant's roots first!

shows a brief sketch of roots growing down into the earth.
Let's use the progression

to reach the character, 入 rù, that means "to enter" in Chinese.

Because 入 looks very similar to the important character 人, so, here is a need to introduce the character 人.

If we see a person at a distance,

it may look like 夨, 夨, 人, 亻, or 人.

So, 亻 symbolizes a person and 人 rén means "person" or "people" in Chinese. Below are the correct forms:

English	one person	two people	three people
Chinese	一人	二人	三人
	1人	2人	3人

You have learned:
一只不走运的狐狸，不小心失足掉入

井 jǐng
well

How do we construct a character that means "well" in Chinese? Let's look at an ancient well first!

蓜 shows an ancient well protected by wooden fence.
Let's use the progression

蓜 ➡ 井 ➡ 井 ➡ 井

to reach the character, 井 jǐng, that means "well" in Chinese.

口 shows a sketch of a mouth, so 口 kǒu means "mouth" or "entrance" in Chinese. Because the entrance of a well looks like "口", so, 口 has been selected as "a character to count wells." Below are the correct forms:

English	one well	two wells	three wells
Chinese	一口井	二口井	三口井
	1口井	2口井	3口井

You have learned:
一只不走运的狐狸，不小心失足掉入一口井
An unlucky Fox incautiously lost its footing and fell into a well.

裏里 lǐ
inside

How do we construct a character that means "inside" in Chinese? Let's look at a rice field first!

⊞ shows an aerial view of a rice field.

田 tián has been selected to mean "a piece of land for growing crops, vegetables, or something else" in Chinese.

土 — Lots of plants growing from the earth
— The surface of the earth
— Earth

The picture above shows the Chinese character 土 tǔ, that means "earth" or "dirt" in Chinese.

Now, by putting 田 on the top of 土, 里 lǐ symbolizes "land for growing crops or vegetables," so 里 has been used to mean "inside," or "neighborhood." 里 is also used as a "unit of length."

⌒ shows the collar of an older style of Chinese clothing.

Let's use the progression

及 ➔ 仌 ➔ 衣

to reach the character, 衣 yī, that means "clothes" in Chinese. 衣 is also used to mean "coating" in Chinese.

Let's use this progression

里+衣 ➔ 里衣 ➔ 裏

to reach the character, 裏 lǐ, that symbolizes "something **inside** the clothes", so, 裏 means "inside." 裏 is a traditional Chinese character. 裏 is 里 in simplified Chinese, however please note that 裏 and 里 also have different meanings and usages.

English	well	inside	inside a well	to fall into a well
Traditional Chinese	井	裏	一口井裏	掉入一口井裏
Simplified Chinese		里	一口井里	掉入一口井里

Note: *As shown below, the Chinese "full stop" (or "." in English), is a small circle "。"*

You have learned:

一只不走运的狐狸，不小心失足掉入一口井里。

An unlucky Fox incautiously lost its footing and fell into a well.

太 tài
excessively; too

How do we construct a character that means "excessively" in Chinese? Let's learn the character "big" in Chinese first!

Ancient Chinese thought the sky, earth, and human were all "big."

𣎴 𣎴 大 大 大 These are brief sketches of a person, with outstretched arms signifying something big. Finally, 大 dà has been selected as the character to mean "big" in Chinese.

If we add one extra "dot" to 大, we get 太 to mean "excessive" or "excessive" in Chinese. Also, 太 tài means "too."

You have learned:
一只不走运的狐狸，不小心失足掉入一口井里。
井太 An unlucky Fox incautiously lost its footing and fell into a well. The well was too

Have you noticed that Chinese verbs don't change as the tense changes? Unlike English, each Chinese verb has only one form, which remains the same in any tense.

深 shēn
depth; deep

How do we construct a character that means "deep" in Chinese? Let's look at the character, 深, directly!

If we break apart the character 深, it contains three parts: 氵, 冖, and 木.
Let's find out the meaning of each part.

Now we will find out what 氵 stands for.

≈ shows a sketch of a river. You can feel the running water in the river.
Let's use the progression:

≈ ➡ ⫶ ➡ 氵

to reach the symbol, 氵, that is usually an indication of liquid or water. When 氵 is used as a component of other characters, these are usually ones that are associated with water or liquid.

Let's use the progression 巛 ➡ 川 ➡ 水
to reach the character, 水 shuǐ, that means "water" in Chinese.

shows the picture of a cave.

冂, 冗, 空, or 穴 is the abstraction or

modification of 🕳. So, 穴 xuè means "a

cave," "a den," "a hole," or "an acupuncture
point" in Chinese.

木 ——— branches growing upwards
   ——— roots

The above shows a brief sketch of a tree.
Let's use this progression

朩 ➜ 朩 ➜ 木 ➜ 朩

to reach the character, 木 mù, that means
"wood" in Chinese.

By putting 氵, 冖, and 木 together, 深
symbolizes "the *depth* of water in a hole,"
because we can use a long stick to check
water depth, so 深 shēn means "depth" or
"deep" in Chinese.

English	water	well	too	deep	The water well is too deep.
Chinese	水	井	太	深	水井太深

You have learned:

一只不走运的狐狸，不小心失足掉入一口井里。
井太深，

An unlucky Fox incautiously lost its footing and fell into
a well. The well was too deep,

無 无 wú
without; nothing

How do we construct a character that means "nothing" in Chinese? Let's look at a cremation scene first!

a corpse ——
a big fire —— 無 —— firewood

Obviously, the corpse disappears after the cremation.

If we see a person at a distance,

it looks like 🚶, 🧍, 人, 亻, 𠂆, or 人.

亻 is often used as a component of a Chinese character to symbolize that this character is related to a human being.

Let's use the progression

無 ➡ 無 ➡ 無 ➡ 無

to reach the character, 無 wú, which means "without" or "nothing."

無 is a traditional Chinese character.

無 is 无 in simplified Chinese.

You have learned:

一只不走运的狐狸，不小心失足掉入一口井里。
井太深，狐狸无

法 fǎ
method; way; law

How do we construct a character that means "way" in Chinese? Let's look at the character 法 directly.

If we break apart the character 法, it contains two parts: 氵 and 去.

Now we will find out what 氵 stands for.

≋ shows a sketch of a river. You could feel the running water in the river.

Let's use the progression

≋ ➤ ⁝ ➤ 氵

to reach the symbol, 氵, that is usually an indication of liquid or water. When 氵 is used as a component of other characters, they are usually these are ones that are associated with water or liquid.

⚓ shows a person leaving a cave or home. Let's use the progression

⚓ ➤ 🔱 ➤ 去

to reach the character, 去 qù, that means "to

leave" or "to go" in Chinese.

浅 shows a person leaving his home and thinking about what's the best **method** or **way** to cross a river ahead.

Let's use the progression

浅 ➜ 浛 ➜ 法

to reach the character, 法 fǎ , that means "method" or "way" in Chinese.

法 is also used to mean "law" in Chinese.

English	without	way	no way
Traditional Chinese	無	法	無法
Simplified Chinese	无		无法

You have learned:

一只不走运的狐狸，不小心失足掉入一口井里。
井太深，狐狸无法

An unlucky Fox incautiously lost its footing and fell into a well. Because the well was too deep, the Fox couldn't

The Fox 🦊 **and The Goat** 🐐

逃 táo
to flee; to escape

How do we construct a character that means "to flee" in Chinese? Let's look at how people run from danger!

灬, 兆, or 兆 shows a brief sketch of "a person running away from danger." It's regarded as an "omen" or "portent" if animals run away from trees. So, 兆 means "omen" or "portent" in Chinese.

⺉ or ⻌ shows a person running so fast that it leaves a dust trail behind him.

By putting ⺄ and 灬 together, 逃 symbolizes "a person running away." Therefore, 逃 táo means "to flee" or "to escape" in Chinese.

You have learned:
一只不走运的狐狸，不小心失足掉入一口井里。
井太深，狐狸无法逃
An unlucky Fox incautiously lost its footing and fell into a well. Because the well was too deep, the Fox couldn't escape

出 chū
exit

How do we construct a character that means "exit" in Chinese? Let's look at a sketch first!

⊥ symbolizes a plant sprouting upward out of the earth.

Let's use the progression ⊥ ➜ ⊻ ➜ 出

to reach the character, 出 chū, that means "exit" in Chinese.

出 can also mean "to produce" or "to issue."

You have learned:
一只不走运的狐狸，不小心失足掉入一口井里。
井太深，狐狸无法逃出
An unlucky Fox incautiously lost its footing and fell into a well. Because the well was too deep, the Fox couldn't escape

The Fox  and The Goat

來 来 lái
to come

How do we construct a character that means "to come" in Chinese? Let's look at a wheat plant first!

, , or shows a sketch of a wheat plant that is ready for harvest, while symbolizes the root. It is at this time that many animals, birds, and people are *drawn* to it.

Let's use the progression → → 來

to reach the character, 來 lái, that means "to come." 來 is a traditional Chinese character. 來 is 来 in simplified Chinese.

English	to come	exit	to come out
Traditional Chinese	來	出	出來
Simplified Chinese	来		出来

You have learned:

一只不走运的狐狸，不小心失足掉入一口井里。
井太深，狐狸无法逃出来。

An unlucky Fox incautiously lost its footing and fell into a well. Because the well was too deep, the Fox couldn't escape the well.

这 这 zhè
this

How do we construct a character that means "this" in Chinese? Let's look at an illustration first.

shows a person walking and pointing at the ground saying, "This is the place." At some point in our lives, it is likely we or someone we know has done this.

The key concepts of the above illustration are: "foot," "walk," "speak," and "***this***."
Let's look directly at the character, 这, that contains the four concepts above. Why?

If we break apart the character 这, it contains two parts: 辶 and 言.

丩亡 shows a sketch of an intersection.
Let's use the progression

丩亡 ➡ 彳 ➡ 彳 ➡ 彡 ➡ 彡

to reach the symbol, 彡, that symbolizes "to

walk" here.

🦶 shows a sketch of a foot.
Let's use the progression

🦶 ➔ 足 ➔ ⻊ ➔ 止

to reach the symbol, 止, that symbolizes
"stop" or "foot" here.

彡 symbolizes "walk" and 止 symbolizes
"stop," therefore 辵 or 辶 symbolizes "to walk
or move intermittently," while 辵 is another
form of 辶, according to ancient Chinese
literature.

😐 shows a sketch of a speaking face.
Let's use the progression 😐 ➔ 言
to reach the character, 言 yán, that means "to
say" or "to speak" in Chinese.

Now by putting 辶 and 言 together, 這 zhè
symbolizes a person walking intermittently and
pointing out something to others while saying,
"***this*** is the place"; therefore, 這 was selected

to mean "this." 這 is a traditional Chinese character. 這 is 这 in simplified Chinese.

English	this fox	
Traditional Chinese	這隻狐狸	這狐狸
Simplified Chinese	这只狐狸	这狐狸

*這狐狸 or 這隻狐狸 is used interchangeably.

English	this well	this water well
Traditional Chinese	這口井	這口水井
Simplified Chinese	这口井	这口水井

English	this small well	this deep well
Traditional Chinese	這口小井	這口深井
Simplified Chinese	这口小井	这口深井

You have learned:

一只不走运的狐狸，不小心失足掉入一口井里。井太深，狐狸无法逃出来。这

An unlucky Fox incautiously lost its footing and fell into a well. Because the well was too deep, the Fox couldn't escape the well.

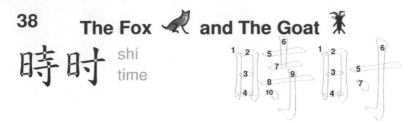
時时 shí
time

How do we construct a character that means "time" in Chinese? Let's look at the character, 時, directly!

If we break apart the character 時, it contains three parts: 日, 士 and 寸.
Let's find out the meaning of each part.

☀ shows a sketch of the sun. If you look at the sun through a pair of very dark sunglasses, the sun may look like ⊙.
Let's use the progression

⊙ ➔ ⊖ ➔ 日 ➔ 日

to reach the character, 日 rì, that means "sun" in Chinese.

☰ symbolized "ten" originally in ancient China.
Let's use the progression

▤ ➜ ▤ ➜ ▮ ➜ ▬ ➜ ┬ ➜ ┼

to reach the character, ┼ shí, that means "ten" in Chinese.

"—" means "one" in Chinese.

Finally, in ancient China, 士 symbolized, "a wise person who was able to count from 1 to 10," so, 士 shì, means, "a learned person," in Chinese. Here, 士 also symbolizes "count."

寸 is related to "pulse-taking," that has been an important element of traditional Chinese medical diagnosis for many years in Chinese society.

🖐 or 🖐 shows the hand and the black dot "•" where the Chinese doctors feel the pulse.
Let's use the progression

🖐 ➜ ⍦ ➜ ⍦ ➜ ⌁ ➜ ┬ ➜ 寸

to reach the character, 寸, that symbolizes "heart" here, because what the doctor gets from the pulse-taking is the beating or throbbing of the heart.

Because culturally Chinese people associate the heart with "the source of thinking" or "mind," so, 寸 symbolizes "mind" here.

And the distance between where the Chinese doctors feels the pulse and the hand is 寸 cùn in Chinese. So, 寸 is "a unit of length equal to one-third of a decimeter" in Chinese.

By putting 日 , 士, and 寸 together, 時 shí symbolizes "a person looking at the sun and counting the *time*," so, 時 shí means "time."

One of the extended meanings of 時 is "hour."

時 is a traditional Chinese character.

時 is 时 in simplified Chinese.

English	at the moment
Traditional Chinese	這時
Simplified Chinese	这时

山 shān
mountain

How do we construct a character that means "mountain" in Chinese? Let's look at a sketch of mountains first!

▲▲▲ shows a brief sketch of mountains.

Let's use the progression ▲▲▲ ➜ 山

to reach the character, 山 shān, that is a general name for "mountain" in Chinese.

English	big	small	big mountain	small mountain
Chinese	大	小	大山	小山

You have learned:

一只不走运的狐狸，不小心失足掉入一口井里。
井太深，狐狸无法逃出来。这时，一只山

An unlucky Fox incautiously lost its footing and fell into a well. Because the well was too deep, the Fox couldn't escape the well. At the moment, a ...

The Fox and The Goat

羊 yáng
a general name for goat and sheep

How do we construct a character to express "a general name for goat or sheep" in Chinese? Let's look at a sketch of a goat first!

shows a brief sketch of a goat with two horns, two ears, four feet, and a tail.
Let's use the progression

to reach the character, 羊 yáng, that is "a general name for goat and sheep" in Chinese.

山羊 means goat in Chinese.

English	mountain	goat	baby goat	big goat
Chinese	山	山羊	小山羊	大山羊

English	this goat
Traditional Chinese	這隻山羊
Simplified Chinese	这只山羊

You have learned:

一只不走运的狐狸，不小心失足掉入一口井里。
井太深，狐狸无法逃出来。这時，一只山羊

An unlucky Fox incautiously lost its footing and fell into a well. Because the well was too deep, the Fox couldn't escape the well. At the moment, a Goat

經 经 jīng
to pass through

How do we construct a character that means "to pass through" in Chinese? Let's look at a sketch of a "loom" first!

蕪 shows a brief sketch of an ancient loom. You can see the vertical yarns passing through the device.
Let's use the progression

蕪 ➔ 巠 ➔ 巠 ➔ 巠

to reach the symbol, 巠 , that symbolizes "to pass through" in Chinese here.

𢇁 shows the drawing of silk thread in ancient China.
Let's use the progression

𢇁 ➔ 糸 ➔ 糸 ➔ 糸

to reach the symbol, 糸 mì or 糸 mì, that symbolizes "a thin thread" or "material for cloth" in Chinese.

When 糸 is used as a component of a Chinese character, it symbolizes that this character is related to the material for cloth.

Now, by putting 糸 and 巠 together, 經 jīng means "the vertical yarns of a fabric." Three of the extended meanings of 經 are "longitude", "experience", and "to pass through."

經 is a traditional Chinese character.

經 is 经 in simplified Chinese.

You have learned:
一只不走运的狐狸，不小心失足掉入一口井里。
井太深，狐狸无法逃出来。这时，一只山羊经
An unlucky Fox incautiously lost its footing and fell into a well. Because the well was too deep, the Fox couldn't escape the well. At the moment, a Goat passed

過 过 guò
passed; mistake

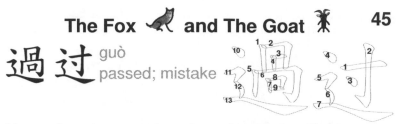

How do we construct a character that means "passed" in Chinese? Let's look at "a mouth with dripping saliva" first!

———— chin

The above shows "a mouth with dripping saliva."
Let's use the progression

to reach the symbol, 咼, that symbolizes "passed" here in Chinese, because the dripping saliva passed by the mouth.

As we learned the character 這 zhè (this), 辶 symbolizes "to walk or move intermittently."

Now, by putting 辶 and 咼 together, 過 guò means "passed." Two of the extended meanings of 過 are "mistake" and "to pass."

Also, 過 indicates "a completion of an action."

過 is a traditional Chinese character.

過 is 过 in simplified Chinese.

English	to pass by
Traditional Chinese	經過
Simplified Chinese	经过

English	a goat passing by
Traditional Chinese	一隻山羊經過
Simplified Chinese	一只山羊经过

過失 means "fault," "error," or "mistake."

過失 are traditional Chinese character.

過失 is 过失 in Simplified Chinese.

You have learned:

一只不走运的狐狸，不小心失足掉入一口井里。
井太深，狐狸无法逃出来。这時，一只山羊经过

An unlucky Fox incautiously lost its footing and fell into
a well. Because the well was too deep, the Fox
couldn't escape the well. At the moment, a Goat
passed by

看見

kàn jiàn
see (something)

看见

How do we construct characters that mean "see (something)" in Chinese? Let's look at how people "watch" first!

As we watch something outdoors, we often use one **hand** to keep the sunlight out of our **eye**s.

◉ shows a sketch of a beautiful eye. Let's use this progression

◉ ➔ ◫ ➔ 目 ➔ 目

to reach the character, 目 mù, that means "eye" in Chinese.

⚘ shows a sketch of a person's hand. Let's use this progression ⚘ ➔ 手
to reach the symbol, 手, which symbolizes "hand."

Now, by putting 手 and 目 together, 看 shows

exactly "a person watching something with his hand above his eye," so, 看 kàn means "to watch" in Chinese.

To avoid employing a one-syllable character in speech, we need to find another character to go with 看 here.

臣 symbolizes a person "watching."
罘 symbolizes "eyesight reaching an end or eyesight reaching something."
Let's use this progression
罘 ➔ 罘 ➔ 見
to reach the character, 見 jiàn, that means eyesight reaching an end or seeing something.

By putting 看 and 見 together, 看見 kàn jiàn means "see (something)."

看見 are traditional Chinese characters.

看見 is 看见 in simplified Chinese.

You have learned:
一只不走运的狐狸，不小心失足掉入一口井里。井太深，狐狸无法逃出来。这时，一只山羊经过看见

了 le
a function character to indicate the end
of an action; finish; understand

How do we construct a character that means "finish" in Chinese? Let's look at a bow!

𝄐 shows a sketch of a bow.
Let's use the progression 𝄐 ➡ 𝄐 ➡ 弓
to reach the character, 弓 gōng, that means "bow" in Chinese.

丿 shows a sketch of an unstrung bow. It happened when a war ended, the warriors were ready to go home.
Let's use the progression
丿 ➡ 丿 ➡ 𝟛 ➡ 了

to reach the character, 了 , that symbolizes the

end of an event. Therefore, 了 le means "finish"

in Chinese. Also, 了 acts as "a function

character to indicate a past tense," or "a

function character to indicate the end of an

action." 了 can also mean "understand."

The Fox and The Goat

問 问 wèn
to ask

How do we construct a character to express "to ask" in Chinese? Let's look at a door first!

shows a sketch of a saloon door.

Let's use the progression 開 ➔ 門 ➔ 門 to reach the character, 門 mén, that means "door" in Chinese.

門 is 门 in simplified Chinese.

口 means "mouth" or "entrance" in Chinese.

By putting 門 and 口 together, 問 symbolizes "someone approaching a door, and opens his mouth," therefore, 問 means "to ask."

問 is a traditional Chinese character.

問 is 问 in simplified Chinese.

English	to ask	fox	ask fox
Traditional Chinese	問	狐狸	問狐狸
Simplified Chinese	问		问狐狸

為什麼

wèi   shén   me

why

为什么

How do we construct characters that mean "why" in Chinese? Let's look at a scene first!

This sketch shows "a person is riding on an elephant and the elephant is doing some kind of work." As a person watches the scene, a question may come up in his mind automatically: "***What*** are they ***do***ing?"

Let's use the progression

to reach the character, 為, that symbolizes "to do (something)" or "is," so, 為 wéi means "to do" or "is." Also, 為 wèi means "reason."

為 is a traditional Chinese character.

為 is 为 in simplified Chinese.

How do we construct characters to mean "what" in Chinese? Let's look at how people count first!

≣ symbolized "ten" originally in ancient China. Later, people used ✚, ✛, or ✜ to symbolize "ten," because people knew better how to tie things together. Finally, the character, 十 shí, has been selected to mean "ten" in Chinese.

If we see a person at a distance, it may look like this: 𝑘, 𝑘, 人, 𝟙, 𝑓, or 𝑓. By putting 𝟙 and 十 together, 𝑓ᵗ, 𝑓ᵗ, or 什 shows a person, 𝟙, carrying ten things of something on his back. Therefore, 什 means "varieties of things" in Chinese.

As we learned the character 深 shēn means "deep" earlier. We also learned 木 mù means "wood" or symbolizes a "tree."

林 lín means "grove" in Chinese.

森 sēn means "forest" in Chinese.

Let's use this symbol, 广 , to represent a cave, a home, or a place, where ancient people could make a home.

In ancient China, people brought fiber crops home, 广 , for further processing to get fiber. So, by putting 广 and 林 together, 麻 means "fiber crops," and one of its extended meanings is "numerous" in Chinese.

🐛 shows a drawing of a baby.
Let's use the progression

🐛 ➜ 8 ➜ Ɛ ➜ ⅀ ➜ 幺

to reach the symbol, 幺 , that symbolizes "small."

By putting 麻 and 幺 together, 麼 me symbolizes "small." 麼 also indicates "a question mark." 麼 is a traditional Chinese character. 麼 is 么 in simplified Chinese.

The Fox 🦊 **and The Goat** 🐐

By putting 什 and 麼 together, 什麼 symbolizes "variety of small things," so it answers the question "**What**?" Therefore, 什麼 shén me means "what."

什麼 are traditional Chinese characters. 什麼 is 什么 in simplified Chinese.

By putting 為, 什, and 麼 together, 為什麼 wèi shén me means "why."

為什麼 are traditional Chinese characters.

為什麼 is 为什么 in simplified Chinese.

English	is	what	for what reason/why?
Traditional Chinese	為	什麼	為什麼?
Simplified Chinese	为	什么	为什么?

You have learned:

一只不走运的狐狸，不小心失足掉入一口井里。井太深，狐狸无法逃出来。这时，一只山羊经过看见了，问狐狸为什么

An unlucky Fox incautiously lost its footing and fell into a well. Because the well was too deep, the Fox couldn't escape the well. At the moment, a Goat passed by and saw the Fox, so the Goat asked why

在 zài
at; in; to exist

How do we construct a character to indicate "at (a location)" in Chinese? Let's read a story first!

One day a woman was hiking in a mountainous area and found a river. She wanted to swim, but there is no need to bring all of her money with her into the water. So she hid her money behind a dirt pile. After one hour, she was wondering whether her money were still there, so she went back to check and touched her money with her hand to make sure her cards were still "present" there safely.

In this story, we mentioned the concept of "existence." The character "在" depicts the above scene. Why?

First let's look at the character 土.

土 ── Lots of plants growing from the earth
── The surface of the earth
── Earth

The picture above shows the Chinese character 土 tǔ, which means "earth" or "dirt" in

Chinese. Also, 土 symbolizes "a dirt pile" here.
凷 symbolizes "something hidden behind a dirt pile."

𐔃 shows a sketch of a hand.
Let's use the progression 𐔃 ➜ ⼌ ➜ ノ
to reach the symbol, ノ, that symbolizes a hand here.

⺋ , 才 or 才 symbolizes "a person's hand touching something" here.

By putting ノ, I, and 土 together, 在 means "at (a location)," "in (a location)," or "to exist" in Chinese.

English	in a location	the inside of the well	inside the well
Traditional Chinese	在	井裏	在井裏
Simplified Chinese		井里	在井里

You have learned:
一只不走运的狐狸，不小心失足掉入一口井里。
井太深，狐狸无法逃出来。这时，一只山羊经过
看见了，问狐狸为什么在

說 说 shuō
to say; to speak

How do we construct a character to express "to say" in Chinese? Let's look at a human face first!

shows a sketch of a speaking face. Let's use the progression ➜ 言

to reach the character, 言 yán, that means "to say" or "to speak" in Chinese. 言 is often used as a component of a Chinese character.

This shows the picture of a person praying to god with several sticks of incense. While praying, this person usually *talk*s to the gods. This scene is often seen at temples in Asia. Let's use the progression

➜ ➜ ➜ 兌

to reach the symbol, 兌, that symbolizes "to speak" here.

By putting 言 and 兌 together, 說 shuō means "to say" or "to speak."

說 is a traditional Chinese character.

說 is 说 in simplified Chinese.

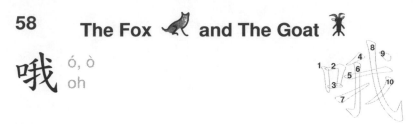

哦 ó, ò
oh

How do we construct a character that means "oh" in Chinese? Let's construct a character to mean "I(我)" in Chinese first!

If we break apart the character 我, it contains two parts: 手 and 戈.

shows a brief sketch of a wheat plant.

hanging grains — 米 — leaves growing upwards
— roots

The above shows an abstraction of 丨.
Let's use this progression

丨 ➔ 米 ➔ 禾 ➔ 禾 ➔ 手

to reach the symbol, 手, which symbolizes "the plant for growing grains" here.

shows an ancient weapon with a tassel at one end. 戈 or 戈 is the symbol of 丨, so 戈 symbolizes a "weapon" and 戈 gē means a "halberd" in Chinese.

By putting 扌 and 戈 together, 我 wǒ symbolizes "**I** guard the plants with a weapon." Accordingly, 我 means "I" or "me" in Chinese. "我的" means "my" or "mine" in Chinese.

口 shows a sketch of a mouth, so, 口 kǒu means "mouth" or "entrance" in Chinese.

By putting 口 and 我 together, 哦 ò or ó seems like "a person opens his mouth and says oh," so, 哦 has been selected to mean "oh" in Chinese.

哦 ó with the rising tone expresses a questioning tone, while 哦 ò with the falling tone expresses surprise. Both are appropriate in the story. It all depends on the speaker's mood or intention.

You have learned:

一只不走运的狐狸，不小心失足掉入一口井里。
井太深，狐狸无法逃出来。这时，一只山羊经过
看见了，问狐狸为什么在井里？狐狸说："哦！

你 nǐ
you

How do we construct a Chinese character that means "you?" Let's look at how Chinese people act while saying "you."

Traditionally, some Chinese point their forefingers to others while saying "you."

👉 , 👆 , or ✍ shows a sketch of a hand gesture.
Let's use the progression

to reach symbol, 尔, that symbolizes "you" here.

Now, let's introduce the character that means "female."

🧍 shows a common symbol for a woman.

Let's use the progression 🧍 ➡ 🧍 ➡ 女

to reach the character, 女 nǚ, that means "woman," "female," or "daughter" in Chinese.

女 is also often used as a component of a character, such as the following 妳.

By putting 女 and 尔 together, 妳 means "you" for a female **in traditional Chinese**.

As we learned earlier, 亻 symbolizes a person. By putting 亻 and 尔 together, 你 means "you" for a male in Chinese.

In the story the goat is regarded as a male. Please note 你 means "you" for both a male and a female in simplified Chinese in China.

English	you(male)	you(female)
Traditional Chinese	你	妳
Simplified Chinese	你	你

🫀, 🫀, 心, or 心 shows a sketch of a heart, and 心 xīn has been chosen to mean "heart" in Chinese.

By putting 心 under 你, 您 nín is the polite way of addressing a person, you, in both traditional and simplified Chinese.

The Fox  and The Goat

知 道   zhī dào
        to know

How do we construct two characters that mean "to know" in Chinese? Let's look at an arrow first!

shows a sketch of an arrow. Let's use the progression

to reach the character, 矢 shǐ*, that means "arrow" in Chinese. 矢 also symbolizes "fast" here.

* *shǐ is onomatopoeia, originating from the sound of a fast flying arrow.*

口 kǒu means "mouth" or "entrance" in Chinese.

By putting 矢 and 口 together, 知 zhī means "to know" in Chinese, because when a person really ***know***s something well, he then may be able to speak fast.

Confucius used this character, 知, while

talking to his students 2500 years ago. For verbal conversation, "知道" is often used to mean "to know" in modern Chinese. Here, let's introduce the character, 道.

首 shows a head, that contains the face and hair, according to ancient Chinese literature. Let's use the progression

首 ➝ 首 ➝ 首

to reach the character, 首 shǒu, which means "a human head" or "an animal head" in Chinese. Often 首 can be used as a component of a Chinese character, such as the following 道.

辶 or 辶 shows a person or a subject moving so fast that it leaves a dust trail behind him or it.

By putting 辶 and 首 together, 道 dào symbolizes "driving a horse-drawn carriage," and at that moment the driver was thinking about "instructing the horse to run on the **road**." Therefore, 道 means "road" in Chinese.

The Fox 🦊 and The Goat 🐐

Several of the extended meanings of 道 are "path," "course," "doctrine," and "Taoism."

By putting 知 and 道 together, 知道 zhīdào means "to know" in Chinese.

English	I	I know.	I don't know.
Chinese	我	我知道	我不知道

English	you	you know.	you don't know.
Chinese	你	你知道	你不知道

不知道 is pronounced bù zhīdào.

You have learned:

一只不走运的狐狸，不小心失足掉入一口井里。
井太深，狐狸无法逃出来。这时，一只山羊经过
看见了，问狐狸为什么在井里？狐狸说："哦！
你不知道

An unlucky Fox incautiously lost its footing and fell into a well. Because the well was too deep, the Fox couldn't escape the well. At the moment, a Goat passed by and saw the Fox, so the Goat asked why the Fox was in the well. The Fox said: "Oh! Don't you know

嗎 吗 ma
a question marker

How do we construct a character to indicate "a question mark" in Chinese? Let's look at a scene first!

A little girl was running towards her mother, crying, and screaming "*mommy*!" The mother would say by instinct "what happened?" The picture of the scene is °𐤊...., while O symbolizes the mother was talking to her child. Let's use the progression

°𐤊.... ➜ °𐤊.... ➜ ....馬 ➜ 嗎 ➜ 吗

to reach the character, 嗎 ma, that indicates "a question mark" at the end of an interrogative sentence.

O or 口 symbolizes a mouth, so, 口 kǒu means "mouth" or "entrance" in Chinese.

嗎 is a traditional Chinese character.

嗎 is 吗 in simplified Chinese.

English	You know.	Do you know?	Don't you know?
Traditional Chinese	你知道	你知道嗎?	你不知道嗎?
Simplified Chinese		你知道吗?	你不知道吗?

You may also be interested in knowing that 馬 means "horse" in Chinese.

🐎 shows a brief sketch of a horse.

🐎, 🐎, or 馬 shows the head of a horse with the bridle to control the horse by the rider.

•••• symbolizes the horse's feet running very fast. Let's use the progression

🐎 ➔ 🐎 ➔ 馬 ➔ 馬

to reach the character, 馬 mǎ, that means "horse."

* You may have noticed that the pronunciation of 嗎 is ma which is the same as the sounds /ma/ in "mama." And the pronunciation of 馬 is mǎ which is almost the same as ma.

馬 is a traditional Chinese character.

馬 is 马 in simplified Chinese.

You have learned:

一只不走运的狐狸，不小心失足掉入一口井里。井太深，狐狸无法逃出来。这时，一只山羊经过看见了，问狐狸为什么在井里？狐狸说："哦！你不知道吗？ An unlucky Fox incautiously lost its footing and fell into a well. Because the well was too deep, the Fox couldn't escape the well. At the moment, a Goat passed by and saw the Fox, so the Goat asked why the Fox was in the well. The Fox said: "Oh! Don't you know?

這兒
zhèr
here

这儿

How do we construct two characters that mean "here" in Chinese? Let's look at the character 兒 first!

兒 shows a brief sketch of a child in ancient Chinese literature. ⊖ shows the unclosed section of the skull of a newborn baby, while 儿 shows a child who crawls and relies on others. Let's use the progression

兒 → 兒 → 兒

to reach the character, 兒 ér, that means "child" or "son." 兒 is a traditional Chinese character. 兒 is 儿 in simplified Chinese.

Earlier we have learned 這 zhè, that means "this." 這 is a traditional Chinese character. 這 is 这 in simplified Chinese.

這兒 has been selected to mean "here" in Chinese, while 兒 acts as a "suffix" placed after 這 to avoid employing a one-syllable character in speech.

* Have noticed that the pronunciation of 兒 is ér which is very close to the /re/ in "here."

The pronunciation of "這兒" becomes zhèr.

這兒 are traditional Chinese characters.

這兒 is 这儿 in simplified Chinese.

** * Check out the other great books in this series available online at www.Amazon.com.

Title	Story
Adventures in Mandarin Chinese Vol 1	The Fox and The Goat ISBN: 1-4392-1812-9
Adventures in Mandarin Chinese Vol 2	Two Men and The Bear ISBN: 1-4392-1813-7
Adventures in Mandarin Chinese Vol 3	The Wind and The Sun ISBN: 1-4392-1814-5
Learning Chinese The Easy Way: Read & Understand The Symbols of Chinese Culture	Two Men and The Bear The Wind and The Sun ISBN: 1-4196-8611-9

快 kuài
quick; soon; happy

How do we construct a character that means "quick" in Chinese? Let's observe how people hold chopsticks!

 shows a sketch of a hand holding a pair of chopsticks while eating a meal.
Let's use the progression

夬 → 夬 → 夬 → 夬 → 夬 → 夬

to reach the symbol, 夬, that symbolizes "a hand holding a pair of chopsticks while eating a meal" here.

While using chopsticks, we must concentrate our mind on the food at that moment. So we have to find a Chinese symbol to mean "mind" too.

As we learned the character ⼼ xīn (heart) earlier, we also learned 忄, that symbolizes "mind" in Chinese, because culturally Chinese people associate the heart with "the source of thinking" or "mind." And 忄 can be used as a component of a character, such as the following 快.

By putting 忄 and 夬 together, 快 seems to show "a person using chopsticks who enjoys eating and feeling *happy*." This person is enjoying himself so much, that time seems to go by quickly, therefore, 快 kuài * means "quick", "soon", or "happy" in Chinese.

* kuài *is onomatopoeia, originating from the sound of chopsticks colliding.*

You have learned:

一只不走运的狐狸，不小心失足掉入一口井里。
井太深，狐狸无法逃出来。这時，一只山羊经过
看见了，问狐狸为什么在井里？狐狸说:"哦!
你不知道吗？这儿快

An unlucky Fox incautiously lost its footing and fell into a well. Because the well was too deep, the Fox couldn't escape the well. At the moment, a Goat passed by and saw the Fox, so the Goat asked why the Fox was in the well. The Fox said: "Oh! Don't you know? Here soon

發生

fā shēng
to happen; to occur

发生

How do we construct two characters that mean "to happen" in Chinese? Let's look at "two hands" first!

shows a sketch of two hands.
Here is the progression

to reach the symbol, , that symbolizes "two hands operating something, such as a bow and arrow, ."

As we learned 了 le (a function character to indicate the end of an action) earlier, we also learned 弓 means "bow."

shows a sketch of an arrow.
Let's use the progression

↑ → ⇟ → ⇧ → 殳

to reach the symbol, 殳, that symbolizes an

"arrow" here. So, ⌄ contains 弓 and 殳.

🏹 or 🏹 symbolizes "taking aim with bow
and arrow."
Let's use the progression

🏹 → 發 → 發

to reach the character, 發 fā*, that means "to

send out." 發 is a traditional Chinese

character. 發 is 发 in simplified Chinese.

*fā *is onomatopoeia, originating from the sound of an
arrow being loosed from a bow.*

However, we need another character to go
with 發 to mean "to happen" in Chinese.

Earlier we learned the character 土 tǔ, that
means "earth" or "dirt" in Chinese.

生 shows plants **grow**ing on earth.
Let's use the progression

$$半 → 生 → 生 → 生$$

to reach the character, 生 shēng, which means "to grow" in Chinese. Some of the other extended meanings of 生 are "to occur" "to produce," "to give birth to," "to live," "life," "uncooked," "not ripe," "unfamiliar," "unprocessed," "student," depending on the phrases or context in which it appears.

By putting 發 and 生 together as a phrase, 發 生 fā shēng means "to happen."

發生 are traditional Chinese characters.

發生 is 发生 in simplified Chinese.

English	soon	to happen	to happen soon
Traditional Chinese	快	發生	快發生
Simplified Chinese		发生	快发生

You have learned:

一只不走运的狐狸，不小心失足掉入一口井里。井太深，狐狸无法逃出来。这時，一只山羊经过看见了，问狐狸为什么在井里？狐狸说："哦！你不知道吗？这儿快发生

旱 hàn
    drought

How do we construct a character that means "drought" in Chinese? Let's observe how people react during a prolonged drought.

or shows a person collecting rainwater or carrying water home in a pot during a *drought*.
Let's use the progression

to reach the symbol, 干, that symbolizes "collecting water" here.

As we learned 時/时 shí (time) earlier, we also learned 日 rì which means "sun" in Chinese. By putting 日 on the top of 干, the character 旱 symbolizes "people even desperately trying to collect rain water in the sun," so, 旱 hàn means "drought" in Chinese.

灾 灾 zhāi
disaster

How do we construct a character that means "disaster" in Chinese? Let's learn the character "fire" first.

is a sketch of a fire.

Let's use this progression ➝ 从 ➝ 火

to reach the character, 火 huǒ*, that means "fire" in Chinese. 火 is also often used as a component of a character, such as the following 灾.

* huǒ *is onomatopoeia, originating from the sound of fire.*

《《 shows the smoke and flames rising after a fire. By putting 《《 on the top of 火, 灾 zhāi means "disaster."

灾 is a traditional Chinese character.

灾 is 灾 in simplified Chinese, because often buildings are burned down in fire and

宀 symbolizes a roof of a building.

As we learned 太 tài (extreme) earlier, we also learned 大 dà, which means "big" in Chinese.

English	big	fire	a big fire	disaster	a disastrous fire
Traditional Chinese	大	火	大火	災	火災
Simplified Chinese				灾	火灾

English	a drought	a severe drought
Traditional Chinese	旱災	大旱災
Simplified Chinese	旱灾	大旱灾

You have learned:

一只不走运的狐狸，不小心失足掉入一口井里。井太深，狐狸无法逃出来。这时，一只山羊经过看见了，问狐狸为什么在井里？狐狸说："哦！你不知道吗？这儿快发生大旱灾，

An unlucky Fox incautiously lost its footing and fell into a well. Because the well was too deep, the Fox couldn't escape the well. At the moment, a Goat passed by and saw the Fox, so the Goat asked why the Fox was in the well. The Fox said: "Oh! Don't you know? There is going to be a severe drought,

跳   tiào
      to jump

How do we construct a character that means "to jump" in Chinese? Let's look first at how people jump!

🕺 shows a sketch of "a person jumping."
Let's use the progression 🕺 ➡ 火 ➡ 兆
to reach the symbol, 兆, that symbolizes "jump" here.

As we learned character 走 zǒu (to walk)
earlier, we also learned 足, that symbolizes a foot in Chinese. Often, 足 is used as a component of a Chinese character, such as the following 跳.

Because the "foot" is used to jump, by putting 足 and 兆 together, 跳 tiào means "to jump" in Chinese.

You have learned:

一只不走运的狐狸，不小心失足掉入一口井里。
井太深，狐狸无法逃出来。这時，一只山羊经过
看见了，问狐狸为什么在井里？狐狸说："哦！你
不知道吗？这儿快发生大旱灾，我跳

進 进 jìn
to enter; into

How do we construct a character that means "to enter" in Chinese? Let's look at a gate first!

⊞ shows a sketch of a gate. And ⊞ shows that a visitor is waiting outside the gate and waving his hand. Notice the head is above the gate.

隹 is the abstraction of ⊞, which symbolizes "waiting to **enter**" here.

⻌ or ⻌ shows a person or a subject moving forward so fast that it leaves a dust trail behind him or it. Usually, ⻌ is usually used as a component of a Chinese character, such as the following 進.

By putting ⻌ and 隹 together, 進 jìn means "to enter" or "into."

進 is a traditional Chinese character.

進 is 进 in simplified Chinese.

English	I	jump	into	well	I jump into the well
Traditional Chinese	我	跳	進	井	我跳進井
Simplified Chinese	我	跳	进	井	我跳进井

English	jump	exit	a water well	jump out of the water well
Chinese	跳	出	水井	跳出水井

As we learned earlier, 看 kàn means "to watch" in Chinese.

看看 kàn kàn means "to take a look," "to look around," or "to examine" in Chinese. In this story, 看看 means "to take a look," because the well is such a small place, usually there is no need to "examine" any further.

You have learned:

一只不走运的狐狸，不小心失足掉入一口井里。井太深，狐狸无法逃出来。这时，一只山羊经过看见了，问狐狸为什么在井里？狐狸说："哦！你不知道吗？这儿快发生大旱灾，我跳进井里看看，

An unlucky Fox incautiously lost its footing and fell into a well. Because the well was too deep, the Fox couldn't escape the well. At the moment, a Goat passed by and saw the Fox, so the Goat asked why the Fox was in the well. The Fox said: "Oh! Don't you know? There is going to be a severe drought, so, I jumped into the well to take a look.

The Fox 🦊 and The Goat 🐐

上 shàng
above; upper

下 xià
below; lower

How do we construct a character that means "above" in Chinese? Let's look at an old symbol first!

In ancient China, ⤴ was the symbol to symbolize "above." Later, people also used ⸗ or ⊥ to symbolize "above." Over time, ⊥ was mixed with ⸗ creating 上 shàng which means "above" or "upper" in Chinese.

Originally, people used the symbol ⊤̣, ⸗, or ⊤ to show something that's "under" another object. Over time, ⊤ was mixed with ⸗ creating 下 xià which means "below" or "lower" in Chinese.

English	downwards	to come	to come down
Traditional Chinese	下	來	下來
Simplified Chinese		来	下来

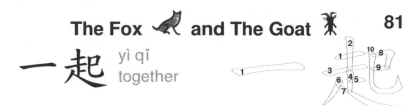
一起 yì qǐ
together

How do we construct two characters that mean "together" in Chinese? Let's look at the Chinese character 起 first!

If we break apart the character, 起, it contains two parts: 走 and 巴. Let's find out the meaning of each part.

shows a brief sketch of a sitting person. Let's use this progression 巴 ➔ 巴 ➔ 巴 to reach the symbol, 巴, that symbolizes "a person in a sitting position" here.

As we learned earlier, the character 走 zǒu means "to walk" or "to leave" in Chinese.

By putting 巴 and 走 together, 起 symbolizes "the process of rising from a sitting position to a walking position." So, 起 qǐ means "to rise up" or "to get up" in Chinese.

一起 symbolizes "to rise up the same time," so, 一起 yì qǐ means "together" in Chinese.

喝   hē
     to drink

How do we construct a character that means "to drink" in Chinese? Let's look at how people drink!

shows a person drinking water.

is an abstract depiction of a person drinking water.

cup ——————
water ——————   —————— face
tongue & throat ——————   —————— mouth

Let's use the progression

to reach the character, 喝 hē, that means "to drink" in Chinese, while 口 means "mouth" or "entrance" in Chinese.

As we learned 深 shēn (deep) earlier, we also learned 水 shuǐ, which means "water" in Chinese.

喝水 means "to drink water" in Chinese.

相信 xiāng xìn
to trust; to believe

How do we construct two characters that mean "to trust" in Chinese? Let's review the character 木 first!

As we learned the character 深 shēn (deep) earlier, we also learned 木 mù, that means wood in Chinese. 木 may also symbolizes "a tree," when 木 acts as a component of a character.

As we learned the character 看 kàn (watch) earlier, we also learned 目 mù, that means eye in Chinese. Here 目 symbolizes "a person."

The act of standing back and *observing* a tree carefully can be expressed with a single Chinese character, 相. And, 相 xiāng has been selected to mean "to examine," in Chinese. Some of the extended meanings of 相 are "appearance," "a phase," "mutual," "mutually," "reciprocal," and "reciprocally."

Now we need to find another character to go with 相 to express "to believe" in Chinese.

If we see a person at a distance,

it looks like 🚶, 👤, 人, 亻, 卜, or 人.

亻 is often used as a component of a Chinese character to symbolize this character is related to "human," such as 信.

As we learned the character 這/这 zhè (this) earlier, we also learned 言 yán, that means "to say" or "to speak." And 言 is often used as a component of a Chinese character, such as the following 信.

Now, by putting 亻 and 言 together, 信 xìn means "to believe" in Chinese, because most people believe in what a person says in ancient time.

Now, by putting 相 and 信 together as a phrase, 相信 xiāng xìn means "to trust" or "to believe" in Chinese, because 相信 symbolizes "to observe then believe."

As we learned earlier, 了 le means "end" in Chinese. 了 also acts as "a function word to indicate the end of an action."

English	goat	to believe	the goat believed
Chinese	山羊	相信	山羊相信了

You have learned:

一只不走运的狐狸，不小心失足掉入一口井里。井太深，狐狸无法逃出来。这时，一只山羊经过看见了，问狐狸为什么在井里？狐狸说："哦！你不知道吗？这儿快发生大旱灾，我跳进井里看看，你为什么不下来一起喝水？"山羊相信了

An unlucky Fox incautiously lost its footing and fell into a well. Because the well was too deep, the Fox couldn't escape the well. At the moment, a Goat passed by and saw the Fox, so the Goat asked why the Fox was in the well. The Fox said: "Oh! Don't you know? There is going to be a severe drought, so, I jumped into the well to take a look. Why don't you come down to drink water with me?" The Goat believed

The Fox and The Goat

話 话 huà
spoken words

How do we construct a character that means "spoken words" in Chinese? Let's observe a tongue first!

shows a brief sketch of a tongue.
Let's use the progression

舌 ➜ 舌 ➜ 舌

to reach the character, 舌 shé, that means tongue in Chinese.

As we learned the character 信 xìn (to believe), we also learned 言 yán, which means "to speak" and 言 is also often used as a component of a Chinese character, such as the following 話.

By putting 言 and 舌 together, 話 huà means "spoken words."

話 is a traditional Chinese character.

話 is 话 in simplified Chinese.

就 jiù
then

How do we construct a character for "then" in Chinese? Let's examine a dog first!

🐕, 犬, or 犬 is a sketch of a dog. You can see the dog's head, black nose, and 4 legs.

So, 犬 quǎn is one of the characters which mean "dog" in Chinese. If 犬 is a normal dog, the character, 尤 yóu, would seem like an outstanding dog to us. So, 尤 means "outstanding" in Chinese.

🏯 shows a **tall** castle or a palace where the emperors lived, and it symbolizes the capital city.

Let's use the progression 🏯 ➡ 京 ➡ 京 to reach the symbol, 京, that symbolizes a "capital," so 京 jīng means "capital" in Chinese.

In a capital city, while looking at a strange dog a thought that may go through a person's mind is "*success*."

If the capital city is old, it may not be what you expected. You may think to yourself, "Oh! I thought it was going to be different, but it's *only* like this," *then* you leave.

So, by putting 京 and 尤 together, 就 jiù can mean "success," "only," or "then" in Chinese.

In this story, 就 means "then."

You have learned:

一只不走运的狐狸，不小心失足掉入一口井里。井太深，狐狸无法逃出来。这時，一只山羊经过看见了，问狐狸为什么在井里？狐狸说："哦！你不知道吗？这儿快发生大旱灾，我跳进井里看看，你为什么不下来一起喝水？"山羊相信了狐狸的話，就跳进井里。

An unlucky Fox incautiously lost its footing and fell into a well. Because the well was too deep, the Fox couldn't escape the well. At the moment, a Goat passed by and saw the Fox, so the Goat asked why the Fox was in the well. The Fox said: "Oh! Don't you know? There is going to be a severe drought, so, I jumped into the well to take a look. Why don't you come down to drink water with me?" The Goat believed Fox's words, then the Goat jumped into the well.

立 刻 lì kè
Immediately

How do we construct two characters that mean "immediately" in Chinese? Let's look at a person first!

Ready to act

大 shows a person and 坕 shows a sketch of a person standing on the ground.

Let's use the progression 坕 ➜ 夳 ➜ 立

to reach the character, 立 lì, that means "stand" in Chinese. One of the extended meanings of 立 is "ready to act."

A short period of time

While coughing, normally we open our mouth then cough, so, 刍, 刈, or 刈 shows a brief sketch of a cough. Another feature of coughing is that it starts from the upper part of the body and comes out of the mouth. In ancient China, ∸ symbolized "above."

By putting ∸ on top of 刍, we get 亥.
Let's use the progression

亥 ➜ 亥 ➜ 亥 ➜ 亥 ➜ 亥

to reach the symbol, 亥, that symbolizes a cough here.

⌐▢ shows a sketch of a Chinese chopping knife. Let's use this progression

⌐▢ → 刀 → ∫ ↓ → ∬ → ∤ → ⺉

to reach the character 刀 and the symbol, ⺉.

刀 dāo means "knife" in Chinese and ⺉ symbolizes "knife." Usually, ⺉ is used as a component of a character, such as the following 刻.

* dāo *is onomatopoeia, originating from the sound of a Chinese chopping knife biting the chopping block.*

While engraving, to some extent, the engraving sound, kè, is similar to the sound of a person coughing; and, like a cough, the engraving sound is very short. Putting 亥 and ⺉ together, 刻 kē has been invented to mean "to engrave" in Chinese. Also ancient Chinese used knives to engrave records of the time passed. They divided a day into 100 parts. Each part was written as, 刻. Now 刻 kè means "15 minutes," or, "a very short period of time" in Chinese.

In conclusion, one of the extended meanings of 立 is "ready to act" and 刻 could mean "a very short period of time." By putting 立 and 刻 together, 立刻 lì kè means "immediately" in Chinese.

English	ready to act	a very short period of time
Chinese	立	刻
English	immediately	
Chinese	立刻	

You have learned:

一只不走运的狐狸，不小心失足掉入一口井里。井太深，狐狸无法逃出来。这时，一只山羊经过看见了，问狐狸为什么在井里？狐狸说："哦！你不知道吗？这儿快发生大旱灾，我跳进井里看看，你为什么不下来一起喝水？"山羊相信了狐狸的话，就跳进井里。狐狸立刻跳上山羊

An unlucky Fox incautiously lost its footing and fell into a well. Because the well was too deep, the Fox couldn't escape the well. At the moment, a Goat passed by and saw the Fox, so the Goat asked why the Fox was in the well. The Fox said: "Oh! Don't you know? There is going to be a severe drought, so, I jumped into the well to take a look. Why don't you come down to drink water with me?" The Goat believed Fox's words, so the Goat jumped into the well. The Fox immediately jumped on the Goat...

The Fox  and The Goat

背 běi, bèi, bēi
back; carry on the back

How do we construct a character that means "the back of a body" in Chinese? Let's look at a sketch of two front line soldiers!

川 or 八 shows two extremely tired soldiers standing or sitting back to back in ancient time. At the moment, enemies came from the **north** of China from time to time.
Let's use the progression

八 ➤ 北 ➤ 北

to reach the character, 北 běi, that means "north" in Chinese.

月 looks like a chunk of pork hanging at a butcher's shop and it also looks like a moon. The moon goes around the earth monthly. So 月 ròu symbolizes "meat," or "flesh," and 月 yuè means "moon" or "month" in Chinese. Here, 月 also symbolizes the shape of human's **back**.

By putting 北 and 月 together, 背 bèi has been selected to mean "back" in Chinese.

* Have you noticed the sound of two people's backs colliding is bèi ?

* English character has different fonts. Chinese character also has different fonts, such as 背 and 背.

English	goat	back	the goat's back
Chinese	山羊	背	山羊的背

English	my	back	my back
Chinese	我的	背	我的背

When 背 acts as a verb to mean "carry on the back" in Chinese, 背 is pronounced bēi.

You have learned:

一只不走运的狐狸，不小心失足掉入一口井里。井太深，狐狸无法逃出来。这时，一只山羊经过看见了，问狐狸为什么在井里？狐狸说："哦！你不知道吗？这儿快发生大旱灾，我跳进井里看看，你为什么不下来一起喝水？"山羊相信了狐狸的话，就跳进井里。狐狸立刻跳上山羊的背，

The Fox 🦊 **and The Goat** 🐐

又 yòu
again

How do we construct a character that means "again" in Chinese? Let's observe birds' behavior first!

Ɂ shows a sketch of a bird taking off from the ground. "Birds of a feather flock together." So, often you may see the second bird taking off from the same area. Therefore, Ɂ symbolizes "again."

Let's use the progression Ɂ ➡ 又 ➡ 又 to reach the character, 又 yòu, that means "again" in Chinese.

English	again	one	to jump	to jump again
Chinese	又	一	跳	又一跳

You have learned:

一只不走运的狐狸，不小心失足掉入一口井里。井太深，狐狸无法逃出来。这时，一只山羊经过看见了，问狐狸为什么在井里？狐狸说:"哦! 你不知道吗？这儿快发生大旱灾，我跳进井里看看，你为什么不下来一起喝水?"山羊相信了狐狸的話，就跳进井里。狐狸立刻跳上山羊的背，又一跳，跳出水井。

再見
再见

zài jiàn
goodbye

How do we construct two characters that mean "goodbye" In Chinese? Let's look at how people dried fish in olden days!

symbolizes fish dried by the sun and wind on a wooden rack. So, symbolizes "many fish" or "repetition" here.
Let's use the progression

to reach the character, 再 zài, that means "again" in Chinese.

shows a sketch of a beautiful eye.
目 means "eye" in Chinese.
symbolizes "watching."
or symbolizes "eyesight reaching an end or eyesight reaching something."
Let's use this progression

to reach the character, 見 jiàn, that means eyesight reaching an end or seeing something. 見 is a traditional Chinese character. 見 is 见 in simplified Chinese.

By putting 再 and 見 together, 再見 zài jiàn is selected to mean "goodbye" or "see…again." 再見 are traditional Chinese characters. 再見 is 再见 in simplified Chinese.

You have learned:

一只不走运的狐狸，不小心失足掉入一口井里。井太深，狐狸无法逃出来。这時，一只山羊经过看见了，问狐狸为什么在井里？狐狸说："哦！你不知道吗？这儿快发生大旱灾，我跳进井里看看，你为什么不下来一起喝水？"山羊相信了狐狸的話，就跳进井里。狐狸立刻跳上山羊的背，又一跳，跳出水井。狐狸说："再见，

An unlucky Fox incautiously lost its footing and fell into a well. Because the well was too deep, the Fox couldn't escape the well. At the moment, a Goat passed by and saw the Fox, so the Goat asked why the Fox was in the well. The Fox said: "Oh! Don't you know? There is going to be a severe drought, so, I jumped into the well to take a look. Why don't you come down to drink water with me?" The Goat believed Fox's words, so the Goat jumped into the well. The Fox immediately jumped on the Goat's back. Then jumped again, the Fox got out of the well. Fox said: "Good-bye,

朋友 péng yǒu
friend

How do we construct two characters that mean "friend" in Chinese? "Friends follows the same leader, and friends work together for the same goal." Let's look at a sketch of a phoenix bird first!

When a phoenix flew in the sky, tens of thousands of other birds came and gathered, according to ancient Chinese literature. Many birds followed the same leader, flew together, and they were *friends*.

showed the above scene in ancient Chinese literature.
Let's use the progression

to reach the character, 朋 péng, which means

"friend." Have you noticed that 月 looks like

the shape of human's back and 朋 looks like

"two friends standing together"?

* You can imagine that the pronunciation of 朋 is almost the same as the sound of phoenix bird flapping its heavy wings.

Also friends go together, because of the same goal. 〄 shows two hands. Here it symbolizes two people work together for the same goal. Let's use the progression

$$ \text{〄} \rightarrow \text{夅} \rightarrow \text{夆} \rightarrow \text{友} \rightarrow \text{友} \rightarrow \text{友} $$

to reach the character, **友** yǒu, which means "friend (work together with others for the same goal)."

By putting **朋** and **友** together, **朋友** péng yǒu means "friend" in modern Chinese.

You have learned:

一只不走运的狐狸，不小心失足掉入一口井里。井太深，狐狸无法逃出来。这時，一只山羊经过看见了，问狐狸为什么在井里？狐狸说："哦！你不知道吗？这儿快发生大旱灾，我跳进井里看看，你为什么不下来一起喝水？"山羊相信了狐狸的話，就跳进井里。狐狸立刻跳上山羊的背，又一跳，跳出水井。狐狸说："再见，朋友！

記 记 ^{jì} to remember

How do we construct a character that means "to remember" in Chinese? Let's look at a belly first!

〉 shows a brief sketch of a person's belly. Let's use the progression

〉 ➡ 〈 ➡ 己 ➡ 己 ➡ 己

to reach the character, 己 jǐ, which means "oneself" in Chinese.

As we learned the character 這/这 zhè (this) earlier, we also learned 言 yán, that means "to say" or "to speak." And 言 is often used as a component of a Chinese character, such as the following 記.

By putting 言 and 己 together, 記 jì means "to remember," because usually "a person can remember what he said by himself."

記 is a traditional Chinese character.

記 is 记 in simplified Chinese.

The Fox and The Goat

住 zhù
to reside; firmly

How do we construct a character that means "to reside" in Chinese? Let's look at a candlestick holder first!

‡ or ‡ shows a sketch of a candlestick holder.
Also, ‡ looks like a light in a house.
‡ Let's use the progression

‡ → ‡ → 主

to reach the character, 主 zhǔ, that stands for "host," "master," "to be in charge of," or "God" in Chinese.

If we see a person at a distance,

it looks like 太, 人, 人, 亻, 卜, or 人.

So, 人 means "person" or "people" in Chinese.

And 亻 is often used as a component of a Chinese character to symbolize this character is related to "human."

By putting 亻 and 主 together, 住 zhù symbolizes "a person sitting beside a light," so 住 means "to reside" in Chinese. It's necessary to hold a candle firmly, so, 住 also means "firm" or "firmly" in Chinese.

When a person seen in a house with a candlelight, he may have stopped his daily work, so 住 also means "to stop" in Chinese. (Because 口 kǒu is a brief sketch of a mouth, 口 means "mouth" or "entrance" in Chinese.) So, "住口！" means "Shut up!" in Chinese.

By putting 記 and 住 together, 記住 jì zhù means "to remember (something) firmly." 記住 are traditional Chinese characters. 記住 is 记住 in simplified Chinese.

English	to memorize	firmly	to memorize (something) firmly
Traditional Chinese	記	住	記住
Simplified Chinese	记		记住

不要   bú yào
     not to

How do we construct two characters that mean "not to" in Chinese? Let's observe a bird in a nest first.

shows a baby bird waiting for feeding.
Let's use the progression

to reach the symbol, 女, that symbolizes "to ask for" here.

symbolizes a mother bird resting or standing in the nest, when the sun sets in the *west* in the evening.
Let's use the progression

to reach the character, 西 xī, that means "west" in Chinese.

By putting 西 on the top of 女, 要 yào means "to ask for" in Chinese. Some of the extended meanings of 要 are "important," "essential," "to want," and "to need." For example, "我要水" means "I want water" or "I need water", depending on the context and the relationship of the two parties who are engaged in the conversation.

不要 bú yào means "not to" in Chinese.

Here, 不 *is pronounced* bú *because* 要 yào *is a fourth-toned character.*

English	remember firmly not to believe.
Traditional Chinese	記住不要相信
Simplified Chinese	记住不要相信

要 is pronounced yāo to mean "to invite," or "to claim."

You have learned:

一只不走运的狐狸，不小心失足掉入一口井里。井太深，狐狸无法逃出来。这时，一只山羊经过看见了，问狐狸为什么在井里？狐狸说："哦！你不知道吗？这儿快发生大旱灾，我跳进井里看看，你为什么不下来一起喝水？"山羊相信了狐狸的話，就跳进井里。狐狸立刻跳上山羊的背，又一跳，跳出水井。狐狸说："再见，我的朋友！记住不要

個 个 gè
a character to
count people

How do we construct a character to count people in Chinese? Let's look at a sketch first.

固 or 固 shows a sketch of a solid object.

So, 固 gù, means "solid" in Chinese.

 This shows a sketch of the human body with internal organs.

Let's use the progression

to reach the symbol, 固, which symbolizes "a human body" here.

If we see a person at a distance, it looks like 𣎴, 𠆢, 人, 亻, 𠂉, or 人.

So, 人 rén means "person" or "people" in Chinese. And 亻 is often used as a component of a Chinese character to symbolize this character is related to "human." By putting 亻 and 固 together, 個 gè has been invented to act as, "a character to count people."

個 is a traditional Chinese character.

個 is 个 in simplified Chinese.

Below are some examples:

English	one person	two people	three people
Traditional Chinese	一個人	二個人	三個人
	1 個人	2 個人	3 個人
Simplified Chinese	一个人	二个人	三个人
	1 个人	2 个人	3 个人

English	one friend	two friends	three friends
Traditional Chinese	一個朋友	二個朋友	三個朋友
	1 個朋友	2 個朋友	3 個朋友
Simplified Chinese	一个朋友	二个朋友	三个朋友
	1 个朋友	2 个朋友	3 个朋友

個 is also used as a classifier* for the numbers of other objects in colloquial or informal Chinese.

* A classifier is a word that denotes the form or shape of an item.

For example, in English we can say a slice of bread or a loaf of bread, but we can't say, "a bread."

Generally, in Chinese all nouns require a classifier just as "bread" does in English.

shēn
body

How do we construct a character that means "body" in Chinese? Let's look at a sketch of a body first!

 showed a human body, according to ancient Chinese literature.
Let's use the progression

to reach the character, 身 shēn, that means "body" in Chinese.

You have learned:
一只不走运的狐狸，不小心失足掉入一口井里。井太深，狐狸无法逃出来。这時，一只山羊经过看见了，问狐狸为什么在井里？狐狸说:"哦！你不知道吗？这儿快发生大旱灾，我跳进井里看看，你为什么不下来一起喝水?"山羊相信了狐狸的話，就跳进井里。狐狸立刻跳上山羊的背，又一跳，跳出水井。狐狸说:"再见，我的朋友！记住不要相信一个身

陷 xiàn
to trap; trapped

How do we construct a character that means "to trap" in Chinese? Let's look at a trap first!

舀 shows a sketch of a person falling into a trap, while 𠂊 symbolizes a person "falling into a trap."

Let's use the progression 舀 ➙ 臽 ➙ 臼

to reach the symbol, 臽, that symbolizes "to trap," and often 臽 is used as a component of another character.

⏝ symbolizes a mountain.
Let's use the progression

⏝ ➙ β ➙ 阝 to reach the symbol, 阝, that symbolizes "a mountain" here.

By putting 阝 and 臽 together, 陷 symbolizes "a person trapped in a mountain area," so, 陷 xiàn means "to trap," "trapped," or "trap" in Chinese.

The Fox  **and The Goat**

困境 kùn jìng
a difficult situation;
predicament

How do we construct two characters that mean "a difficult position" in Chinese? Let's see how to trap a wild animal in a cave first!

🕳 or ⌂ shows a cave for an animal. One way to trap an animal in the cave is to put wooden bars at the cave entrance.

As we learned the character 深 shēn (deep) earlier, we also learned 木 mù, that means "wood" and 木 also often symbolizes "a tree" or "wood", when 木 acts as a component of a character, such as the following 困.

田 symbolizes wooden bars at the cave entrance.

Let's use the progression 田 ➜ 田 ➜ 困 to reach the character, 困 kùn, that means "besieged," "to besiege," "difficult," or "in difficulties" in Chinese.

Now we will try to construct a character to mean "condition" in Chinese? Let's look at a sketch of a gong first!

 This shows a sketch of a gong.

Let's use the progression

囫 ➔ 묘 ➔ 亭 ➔ 音 ➔ 音

to reach the character, 音 yīn, that symbolizes

"a gong," and 音 means "sound" in Chinese, because a gong was a loud and important instrument to produce sound in ancient times.

By putting 音 on the top of 八, 竟 symbolizes "a sound that has come to an end."
Let's use this progression 竟 ➔ 竟

to reach the character, 竟 jìng, that means "to complete," "eventually," or "unexpectedly" in Chinese.

Earlier we learned 土 tǔ, that means "earth" or "dirt" in Chinese. 土 can be used as a component of a character, such as the following 境.

By putting 土 and 竟 together, 境 symbolizes "the end of land", so, 境 could have the following meanings: "border," "boundary," "circumstances," "situation" in Chinese. Usually, 境 go with other character(s) to form a phrase.

困境 kùn jìng means "a difficult situation" or "predicament" in Chinese.

English	in difficulties	situation	in a difficult situation
Chinese	困	境	困境

English	body	trapped	trapped in a difficult situation
Chinese	身	陷	身陷困境

You have learned:

一只不走运的狐狸，不小心失足掉入一口井里。井太深，狐狸无法逃出来。这時，一只山羊经过看见了，问狐狸为什么在井里？狐狸说："哦！你不知道吗？这儿快发生大旱灾，我跳进井里看看，你为什么不下来一起喝水？"山羊相信了狐狸的話，就跳进井里。狐狸立刻跳上山羊的背，又一跳，跳出水井。狐狸说："再见，我的朋友！记住不要相信一个身陷困境

中 zhòng, zhōng
center; in the middle of

How do we construct a character that means "center" in Chinese? Let's look for the symbol of an arrow hitting its target!

shows an arrow that hits its target.

Let's use the progression ⭕➤ → 中 → 中 to reach the character, 中 zhòng*, that means "to hit the target" in Chinese.

* zhòng *is onomatopoeia, originating from the sound of an arrow that hits its target.*

中 zhōng, with a first tone, means "center" or "in the middle of" in Chinese.

English	a fox trapped in the middle of a difficult situation
Traditional Chinese	一個身陷困境中的狐狸
Simplified Chinese	一个身陷困境中的狐狸

The Fox 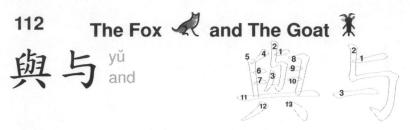 and The Goat

與 与 yǔ
and

How do we construct a character to express "and" in Chinese? Let's observe, "how people work together!"

Ψ shows a sketch of a plant.

Ψ shows a sketch of a plant in a field "—."

shows two people, **A** and **B**, are doing

something for a plant together, and symbolizes "and" or "participation."
Let's use the progression

→ → → → 與

to reach the character, 與 yǔ, that means "and."

與 is a traditional Chinese character.

與 is 与 in simplified Chinese.

English	the fox and the goat
Traditional Chinese	狐狸與山羊
Simplified Chinese	狐狸与山羊

Title: <u>狐狸與山羊</u>(Traditional Chinese)

一隻不走運的狐狸，不小心失足掉入一口井裏。井太深，狐狸無法逃出來。這時，一隻山羊經過看見了，問狐狸爲什麼在井裏？狐狸說："哦！你不知道嗎？這兒快發生大旱災，我跳進井裏看看，你爲什麼不下來一起喝水？"山羊相信了狐狸的話，就跳進井裏。狐狸立刻跳上山羊的背，又一跳，跳出水井。狐狸說："再見，我的朋友！記住不要相信一個身陷困境中的狐狸。"

Title: <u>狐狸与山羊</u>(Simplified Chinese)
(Simplified Chinese is used in China.)

一只不走运的狐狸，不小心失足掉入一口井里。井太深，狐狸无法逃出来。这时，一只山羊经过看见了，问狐狸为什么在井里？狐狸说："哦！你不知道吗？这儿快发生大旱灾， 我跳进井里看看，你为什么不下来一起喝水？"山羊相信了狐狸的话，就跳进井里。狐狸立刻跳上山羊的背，又一跳，跳出水井。狐狸说："再见，我的朋友！记住不要相信一个身陷困境中的狐狸。"

The Fox 🦊 and The Goat 🐐

Title: The Fox and The Goat

An unlucky Fox incautiously lost its footing and fell into a well. Because the well was too deep, the Fox couldn't escape the well.

At the moment, a Goat passed by and saw the Fox, so the Goat asked why the Fox was in the well.

"Oh! Don't you know?" said the Fox, "There is going to be a severe drought, so, I jumped into the well to take a look. Why don't you come down to drink water with me?" The Goat believed the Fox's words, so the Goat jumped into the well.

The Fox immediately jumped on the Goat's back. Then jumping again, the Fox got out of the well. "Good-bye, my friend!" said the Fox, "Remember! Never believe a fox trapped in the middle of a difficult situation."

Pronunciation Reference

The Fox and The Goat

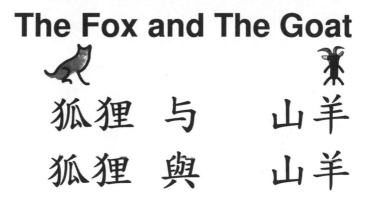

狐狸 与 山羊

狐狸 與 山羊

★ Unveil

the foundation of

Chinese characters!

Pronunciation Reference

(TC: Traditional Chinese   SC: Simplified Chinese   MPS: Mandarin Phonetic System)

Page	TC	SC	Pinyin	Tone	MPS
3	一		yī, yí, yì	1,2,4	ㄧ, ㄧˊ, ㄧˋ
4	二		èr, liǎng	4,3	ㄦˋ, ㄌㄧㄤˇ
4	三		sān	1	ㄙㄢ
5	隻	只	zhī	1	ㄓ
7	狐		hú	2	ㄏㄨˊ
8	狸		lí	2	ㄌㄧˊ
8	里		lǐ	3	ㄌㄧˇ
9	瓜		guā	1	ㄍㄨㄚ
10	卜		bǔ	3	ㄅㄨˇ
10	不		bù, bú	4,2	ㄅㄨˋ, ㄅㄨˊ
11	走		zǒu	3	ㄗㄡˇ
12	運	运	yùn	4	ㄩㄣˋ
12	車	车	chē	1	ㄔㄜ
12	軍	军	jūn	1	ㄐㄩㄣ
14	的		de	5	ㄅㄜ·

The Fox and The Goat
Pronunciation Reference

(TC: Traditional Chinese   SC: Simplified Chinese   MPS: Mandarin Phonetic System)

Page	TC	SC	Pinyin	Tone	MPS
15	白		bái	2	ㄅㄞˊ
15	勺		sháo	2	ㄕㄠˊ
17	小		xiǎo	3	ㄒㄧㄠˇ
18	心		xīn	1	ㄒㄧㄣ
19	失		shī	1	ㄕ
20	足		zú	2	ㄗㄨˊ
21	掉		diào	4	ㄉㄧㄠˋ
22	入		rù	4	ㄖㄨˋ
22	人		rén	2	ㄖㄣˊ
23	井		jǐng	3	ㄐㄧㄥˇ
23	口		kǒu	3	ㄎㄡˇ
24	裏	里	lǐ	3	ㄌㄧˇ
24	田		tián	2	ㄊㄧㄢˊ
24	土		tǔ	3	ㄊㄨˇ
25	衣		yī	1	ㄧ

Pronunciation Reference

(TC: Traditional Chinese   SC: Simplified Chinese   MPS: Mandarin Phonetic System)

Page	TC	SC	Pinyin	Tone	MPS
26	太		tài	4	ㄊㄞˋ
26	大		dà	4	ㄉㄚˋ
27	深		shēn	1	ㄕㄣ
27	水		shuǐ	3	ㄕㄨㄟˇ
28	穴		xuè	4	ㄒㄩㄝˋ
28	木		mù	4	ㄇㄨˋ
29	無	无	wú	2	ㄨˊ
30	法		fǎ	3	ㄈㄚˇ
30	去		qù	4	ㄑㄩˋ
32	逃		táo	2	ㄊㄠˊ
32	兆		zhào	4	ㄓㄠˋ
33	出		chū	1	ㄔㄨ
34	來	来	lái	2	ㄌㄞˊ
35	這	这	zhè	4	ㄓㄜˋ
36	言		yán	2	ㄧㄢˊ

The Fox 🦊 and The Goat 🐐
Pronunciation Reference

(TC: Traditional Chinese   SC: Simplified Chinese   MPS: Mandarin Phonetic System)

Page	TC	SC	Pinyin	Tone	MPS
38	時	时	shí	2	ㄕˊ
38	日		rì	4	ㄖˋ
39	十		shí	2	ㄕˊ
39	士		shì	4	ㄕˋ
39	寸		cùn	4	ㄘㄨㄣˋ
41	山		shān	1	ㄕㄢ
42	羊		yáng	2	ㄧㄤˊ
43	經	经	jīng	1	ㄐㄧㄥ
43	糸		mì	4	ㄇㄧˋ
45	過	过	guò	4	ㄍㄨㄛˋ
47	看		kàn	4	ㄎㄢˋ
47	見	见	jiàn	4	ㄐㄧㄢˋ
47	目		mù	4	ㄇㄨˋ
49	了		le	5	ㄌㄜ˙
49	弓		gōng	1	ㄍㄨㄥ

Pronunciation Reference

(TC: Traditional Chinese   SC: Simplified Chinese   MPS: Mandarin Phonetic System)

Page	TC	SC	Pinyin	Tone	MPS
50	問	问	wèn	4	ㄨㄣˋ
51	為	为	wèi, wéi	4,2	ㄨㄟˋ, ㄨㄟˊ
51	什		shén	2	ㄕㄣˊ
51	麼	么	me	5	ㄇㄜ·
52	林		lín	2	ㄌㄧㄣˊ
52	森		sēn	1	ㄙㄣˊ
53	麻		má	2	ㄇㄚ
55	在		zài	4	ㄗㄞˋ
57	說	说	shuō	1	ㄕㄨㄛ
58	哦		ò, ó	4,2	ㄛˋ, ㄛˊ
58	我		wǒ	3	ㄨㄛˇ ˊ
58	戈		gē	1	ㄍㄜ
60	你		nǐ	3	ㄋㄧˇ
60	女		nǔ	3	ㄋㄩˇ
61	您		nín	2	ㄋㄧㄣˊ

Pronunciation Reference

(TC: Traditional Chinese   SC: Simplified Chinese   MPS: Mandarin Phonetic System)

Page	TC	SC	Pinyin	Tone	MPS
62	知		zhī	1	ㄓ
62	矢		shǐ	3	ㄕˇ
62	道		dào	4	ㄉㄠˋ
63	首		shǒu	3	ㄕㄡˇ
65	嗎	吗	ma	5	ㄇㄚ·
65	馬	马	mǎ	3	ㄇㄚˇ
67	兒	儿	ér	2	ㄦˊ
67	這兒	这儿	zhèr	4	ㄓㄜˋㄦ·
69	快		kuài	4	ㄎㄨㄞˋ
71	發	发	fā	1	ㄈㄚ
72	生		shēng	1	ㄕㄥ
74	旱		hàn	4	ㄏㄢˋ
75	災	灾	zhāi	1	ㄓㄞ
75	火		huǒ	3	ㄏㄨㄛˇ

Pronunciation Reference

(TC: Traditional Chinese   SC: Simplified Chinese   MPS: Mandarin Phonetic System)

Page	TC	SC	Pinyin	Tone	MPS
77	跳		tiào	4	ㄊㄧㄠˋ
78	進	进	jìn	4	ㄐㄧㄣˋ
80	上		shàng	4	ㄕㄤˋ
80	下		xià	4	ㄒㄧㄚˋ
81	起		qǐ	3	ㄑㄧˇ
82	喝		hē	1	ㄏㄜ
83	相		xiāng	1	ㄒㄧㄤ
83	信		xìn	4	ㄒㄧㄣˋ
86	話	话	huà	4	ㄏㄨㄚˋ
86	舌		shé	2	ㄕㄜˊ
87	就		jiù	4	ㄐㄧㄡˋ
87	犬		quǎn	3	ㄑㄩㄢˇ
87	尤		yóu	2	ㄧㄡˊ
87	京		jīng	1	ㄐㄧㄥ
89	立		lì	4	ㄌㄧˋ

The Fox 🦊 and The Goat 🐐
Pronunciation Reference

(TC: Traditional Chinese   SC: Simplified Chinese   MPS: Mandarin Phonetic System)

Page	TC	SC	Pinyin	Tone	MPS
89	刻		kē, kè	1,4	ㄎㄜ,ㄎㄜˋ
90	刀		dāo	1	ㄉㄠ
92	背		běi, bèi, bēi	3,4,1	ㄅㄟˇ, ㄅㄟˋ,ㄅㄟ
92	北		běi	3	ㄅㄟˇ
92	月		ròu, yuè	4,4	ㄖㄡˋ,ㄩㄝˋ
94	又		yòu	4	ㄧㄡˋ
95	再		zài	4	ㄗㄞˋ
97	朋		péng	2	ㄆㄥˊ
97	友		yǒu	3	ㄧㄡˇ
99	記	记	jì	4	ㄐㄧˋ
99	己		jǐ	3	ㄐㄧˇ
100	住		zhù	4	ㄓㄨˋ
100	主		zhǔ	3	ㄓㄨˇ
102	要		yào, yāo	4,1	ㄧㄠˋ, ㄧㄠ
102	西		xī	1	ㄒㄧ

Pronunciation Reference

(TC: Traditional Chinese   SC: Simplified Chinese   MPS: Mandarin Phonetic System)

Page	TC	SC	Pinyin	Tone	MPS
104	個	个	gè	4	ㄍㄜˋ
104	固		gù	4	ㄍㄨˋ
106	身		shēn	1	ㄕㄣ
107	陷		xiàn	4	ㄒㄧㄢˋ
108	困		kùn	4	ㄎㄨㄣˋ
108	境		jìng	4	ㄐㄧㄥˋ
109	音		yīn	1	ㄧㄣ
109	竟		jìng	4	ㄐㄧㄥˋ
111	中		zhòng, zhōng	4,1	ㄓㄨㄥˋ, ㄓㄨㄥ
112	與	与	yǔ	3	ㄩˇ